STRESS OR SANITY

by Sherrie Weaver

Cover Design by Design Dynamics, Glen Ellyn, IL
Typography by Roy Honegger

Published by Great Quotations Publishing Co.,
Glendale Heights, IL

Library of Congress Catalog Card Number: 96-76130

ISBN 1-56245-263-0

Printed in Hong Kong

STRESS OR SANITY

A family getaway is a great idea!
When can I get away from mine?

STRESS OR SANITY

I can't be overdrawn,
I still have checks left.

4

STRESS OR SANITY

To get a driver's license,
you have to take a driver's test.
So how come you don't have
to take a test to get a
marriage license?

STRESS OR SANITY

Into each Wife,
a little strain must fall.

STRESS OR SANITY

Yesterday's stress is past tense.

STRESS OR SANITY

It's mid-December. Do you know
where your credit cards are?

STRESS OR SANITY

I used to be full of the wonder
of it all. Now I'm just full of it.

STRESS OR **SANITY**

You know it's going to be
a bad day when the picture
on the milk carton is yours.

STRESS OR SANITY

Maybe your reality check will clear.

STRESS **OR** SANITY

Don't feel too bad. You still have
everything you had when you
were 17. It's just a foot lower
than it used to be.

STRESS OR SANITY

The ones who have the gold, make the rules. The rest of us just kiss brass.

13

STRESS OR SANITY

Used to be that my true love
brought me chocolate.
Now, my true love IS chocolate.

STRESS OR SANITY

Why do fools fall in love, and
then spend every waking moment
telling you every tedious detail?

17

Stress test: The odds of a piece of toast landing jelly side down are:

a. 50/50
b. not a factor if you have tile
c. directly proportional to the cost of the carpet

STRESS OR SANITY

#4 on the Best Stressed List:
The man whose wife just said
'Happy Anniversary, Honey',
and it was a total surprise.

19

STRESS OR SANITY

The proper response to
"Good Morning" is not "Prove it."

20

STRESS OR SANITY

You know it's going to be a
bad day when your boss refers to
your paycheck as 'the comic strip'.

21

STRESS OR SANITY

Life is full of ups and downs.
I keep hoping my skin will clear up
and my weight will go down.

22

STRESS OR **SANITY**

If you're going to run with
the big dogs, you're going
to get stuff on your shoes.

23

**The bad news? Disco is back.
The worse news? You've still
got the outfit for it.**

STRESS OR SANITY

Remember the saying,
'This too shall pass'?
How come the guy riding your
back bumper never heard it?

Once you pass age 40, your
'big break' will probably be a bone.

STRESS ⊕ SANITY

I still go out frequently. Of course,
now I do it in pieces...my back...
my neck...my knee....

Life is a piece of cake.
And I'm on a strict diet.

STRESS OR SANITY

It's no problem to stretch
the household budget.
Just write rubber checks.

29

STRESS OR SANITY

Tension: Realizing you've just run out of birth control pills. Stress: Your teenage daughter offering to loan you some.

30

STRESS OR SANITY

Being married is like eating
ice cream with chopsticks.
It can be done, if you're careful,
but it doesn't prove anything.

Why do they call it the 'rat race' when the rats are smart enough to avoid it?

STRESS OR SANITY

Behind every dark cloud, there is a really happy car wash owner.

33

STRESS ⊙ SANITY

We spend two years teaching our children to talk. And the next 15 trying to shut them up.

34

STRESS OR SANITY

If you have extra time on your hands, please wipe some off on me.

35

STRESS OR SANITY

The bad news? Your son just went off to college. The worse news? He took your checkbook with him.

36

STRESS OR SANITY

Do taxicab drivers take their work home with them?

37

STRESS OR SANITY

You have to take the bad with
the good. But you can certainly
gripe about the proportions.

STRESS OR SANITY

There's no such thing as a
free lunch. Unless you can talk
somebody else into picking
up the tab.

39

STRESS OR SANITY

Money talks.
My wallet is whispering.

40

Cheer up. Even the majestic oak tree started as a little nut.

STRESS or SANITY

A headcold at your kid's daycare:
Days of Whine & Noses.

42

STRESS OR SANITY

People would not fall in love,
if it were more clearly marked.

43

STRESS OR SANITY

It doesn't get any better than this.
That's what I'm afraid of.

44

STRESS OR SANITY

The calm before the storm means that the power will soon be out.

45

STRESS OR SANITY

People who burn the candle at
both ends are rarely invited
to birthday parties.

46

STRESS OR **SANITY**

Who knows what evil lurks
in the hearts of men?
Their wives, generally.

47

STRESS OR SANITY

You know it's going to be a bad day when you're an hour late for work, and nobody notices.

48

STRESS OR SANITY

Many are called, but few actually return the message.

49

STRESS OR SANITY

76% of people polled said that if they were given an extra hour every day, they would use it to sleep. The other 24% were too busy to answer.

50

STRESS OR SANITY

It was announced today that if you are a white rat, scientists are hazardous to your health.

STRESS OR SANITY

This meeting is just killing time.
By boring it to death.

52

STRESS OR SANITY

Not every one can be a star.
Some of us are just black holes.

53

STRESS OR SANITY

It's a dog eat dog world. And we're all wearing beef bone perfume.

54

STRESS OR SANITY

Smooth sailing means your
boat motor has quit.

55

STRESS OR SANITY

You're not getting older.
You're getting deeper in debt.

56

STRESS OR SANITY

My mind is wandering because
it doesn't have anywhere
specific to go.

57

STRESS OR SANITY

I want a day off from my life.
Just one. I promise I'll be in
all the earlier tomorrow.

58

STRESS OR SANITY

Let me get this straight:
You fire me, I stay home,
collect unemployment,
and watch television.
Sounds good, let's do it.

59

Tension: The 6'4" biker whose motorcycle you just backed into. Stress: His five angry friends.

STRESS OR SANITY

When the going gets tough...
stay home, for heaven's sake!

61

**Life is a bowl of cherries:
Overpriced and only available
at certain times.**

STRESS OR SANITY

**Tension: Starting a new job.
Stress: Being introduced
as 'fresh meat'.**

63

STRESS OR SANITY

The really scary part is that
someday, these will be
the 'good old days'.

64

STRESS OR SANITY

Tension: Getting the invitation for your 20 year high school reunion. Stress: Realizing you still haven't done anything worthwhile.

65

STRESS OR SANITY

One time you don't want to be right: "Honey, I think I left the water running in the tub."

STRESS OR SANITY

#54 on the Best Stressed List:
The mother whose son just
received a drum set for Christmas.

67

**Did Thomas Edison
ever lighten up?**

68

STRESS or SANITY

It could be worse...It could be Monday. If it already is Monday, just give up and go home now.

69

STRESS OR SANITY

You can tell it's going to be a bad day when you discover that not only did the new puppy food not agree with the dog's digestive system, but your carpet cleaner is not up to par.

70

STRESS **OR** SANITY

**Stress is realizing that not only
do you look your actual age,
but you feel it, too.**

STRESS OR SANITY

The good news: You have a
legitimate excuse for not
going to work today.
The bad news: Your excuse is
that you've been fired.

STRESS OR SANITY

It's always something.
And it's generally expensive.

73

STRESS OR SANITY

The good news: You get a decent
income tax refund this year.
The bad news: You still owe
for last year's taxes.

74

Tension: Realizing that you forgot to put a stamp on the mortgage payment.
Stress: Realizing that you also forgot to put a return address on the envelope.

75

STRESS OR SANITY

What if your mother really was
right? About everything?

76

STRESS OR SANITY

Some are born to greatness, others have greatness thrust upon them. Most of us just read about it.

77

STRESS OR SANITY

Mending the clothes: Whatever you sew, that shall you also rip.

78

STRESS OR SANITY

Two kids, two beginning band concerts. On the same night.

79

STRESS OR SANITY

You know it's going to be a bad day when your child gets carsick. And you discover it in the fast lane, halfway between home and the daycare.

80

STRESS OR SANITY

Your ironing basket:
Proof that what goes up does
not necessarily go down.

STRESS OR SANITY

If ignorance is bliss, how come
my boss isn't in a better mood?

82

STRESS OR SANITY

Talk is cheap. That is why so many people do so much of it.

83

STRESS OR SANITY

All good things must come to an
end. Unless somebody thought
to syndicate the re-runs.

84

STRESS or SANITY

'We shall overcome':
The motto of the bonehead
riding your back bumper.

85

**Angoraphobia:
The fear of fuzzy sweaters.**

86

STRESS OR **SANITY**

Walk a mile in another man's shoes, and he'll at least make you polish them.

STRESS OR SANITY

How can I possibly owe income tax?
I didn't make any money last year.

88

**A teenager in the kitchen:
Leader of the Snack.**

STRESS OR SANITY

The course of true love never did run smooth. The state highway department must have taken it over.

90

STRESS OR SANITY

Fortune favors the foolish.
Explains a lot about your family,
doesn't it?

91

STRESS OR SANITY

If you can't beat 'em...the eggs
you bought are way too old to use.

92

STRESS OR SANITY

A cold passed freely between officemates: Unchained Malady.

STRESS _{OR} SANITY

'A happily married couple':
Two people who haven't
been together very long.

94

STRESS OR SANITY

You can't please everyone.
But it is possible to make 'em
all mad at the same time.

95

STRESS OR SANITY

If life is a cabaret, why isn't there a two drink minimum?

96

STRESS OR SANITY

If you can't say something nice
about someone, marry them.

97

Formal dinner party at the boss' house: Time to stress up.

STRESS OR SANITY

The amount of snowfall you receive
will be directly proportional to the
ease of locating your shovel.

99

**Don't worry about tomorrow.
Today will probably do you in.**

**I had an idea.
But it died of loneliness.**

STRESS OR SANITY

I had a thought. Beginner's luck.

102

STRESS OR SANITY

It's time to clean the pot
when the term 'coffee break'
can be taken literally.

103

STRESS OR SANITY

We cannot have a meeting of the minds. You do not have the equipment for it.

104

STRESS OR SANITY

If you keep hanging on by your
fingernails, you'll need a manicure.

105

STRESS OR SANITY

The good do not die young.
But they rarely go anywhere
on a Saturday night.

106

STRESS OR SANITY

Blessed are the cheesemakers.
For they shall get their whey.

107

STRESS or SANITY

There are not enough hours in the day. Unless you get stuck at the Department of Motor Vehicles.

108

STRESS **OR** SANITY

I'm on the corporate weight
loss program. I'm downsizing.

109

STRESS OR SANITY

Most people's hindsight is 20/20,
because most people's 'hinds'
are really easy to see.

110

STRESS OR SANITY

That new employee is so bright,
the boss calls him 'son'.

111

STRESS OR SANITY

Keep your chin up, and you'll bang your head on the door frame.

112

STRESS OR **SANITY**

If you're not the lead dog,
chew your way out of the harness
and make a break for it.

STRESS or SANITY

My boss must think I'm a rose.
He keeps shoveling fertilizer
on me, and cutting me back
when I start to bloom.

STRESS OR SANITY

Living is easy. It's cleaning up
the mess that's the problem.

115

STRESS or SANITY

I don't worry about my kids
running with the wrong crowd.
They'd have to get up off
the couch first.

116

STRESS OR SANITY

Let's review: We get up real early, fight traffic and other cranky commuters to spend all day long at a place we hate. Am I missing something?

117

STRESS OR SANITY

No, you haven't lost your mind.
You dropped it in the gutter.

118

STRESS OR SANITY

It is difficult to climb the corporate
ladder if you're wearing a skirt.

119

STRESS OR SANITY

My boss and I had a battle of wits.
He ran out of ammunition.

STRESS OR **SANITY**

Don't honk your horn at the person in front of you. It can be dangerous to wake up a sleepwalker.

121

STRESS ⓞⓡ SANITY

Beauty is only skin deep. But
stupid goes all the way through.

122

STRESS OR SANITY

You can be pretty sure it's going to be a bad day if your desk calendar has a skull and crossbones drawn through it.

123

STRESS OR **SANITY**

Don't worry about cleaning your desk off. Just wait until it's declared a Superfund site, and use the federal grant money to take a long vacation.

124

STRESS OR SANITY

Don't worry. Make somebody else worry instead.

125

STRESS OR SANITY

**Why do they call them
'Civil Servants' when usually,
they're neither?**

126

STRESS OR SANITY

Parents' stress level is directly proportional to the number of children they have. And how many of them are toilet trained!

127

STRESS OR SANITY

**Permanent Stress:
Never needs ironing.**

128

STRESS OR SANITY

Stress is waking up with a warm, furry body next to you, and you don't have a pet!

129

Only bald men don't have bad hair days.

STRESS OR SANITY

Henry Ford was a driven man.

131

Commuter: Latin word meaning, "to park on the freeway".

132

STRESS OR SANITY

Stressful Situation #14: The engine in your car is making an odd noise, and you can't find the cat.

133

STRESS OR SANITY

A great many people confuse
their lack of planning with
your emergency.

134

STRESS OR SANITY

A fool and his money are never
around when you need them.

135

**Staff Meeting: gathering
of infectious bacteria.**

STRESS OR SANITY

When you have nothing to lose,
you have nothing to worry about.

STRESS or SANITY

Mowing the lawn, raking the leaves, shoveling the walk, tending the garden...
Nature is a lot of work.

138

STRESS OR SANITY

Too much to do, too little time
to do it and too late
to change careers.

139

STRESS OR SANITY

**#39 on the Best Stressed List:
The guy whose dentist's motto is
'No Pain, No Gain'.**

140

STRESS or SANITY

Stress is trying to keep your head
above water, and somebody
else is making waves.

STRESS or SANITY

The key to happiness is
stuck in the lock.

142

STRESS OR SANITY

Love is blind—
and it's not too bright, either.

143

STRESS OR SANITY

Stress Management: What many employees like to do on purpose.

144

Even ministers have to work weekends.

145

STRESS OR SANITY

Life, unlike Algebra, does not have
the answers to the odd problems
in the back of the book.

146

Time Management: An employee's time belongs to management.

E = mc²
(Energy = morning
x 2 cups of coffee)

STRESS OR SANITY

A business person's three favorite words are, "And in conclusion..."

**Stressful situation #24:
A house full of in-laws and
a stopped up toilet.**

STRESS OR SANITY

With pagers, answering machines
and cellular phones, it is now
possible to be interrupted
wherever you go.
Isn't technology wonderful?

151

STRESS OR SANITY

Do unto others.
Then bill them for it.

152

STRESS OR SANITY

Early for bed, early to rise,
will not give you enough time
for everything you need to do.

153

STRESS OR SANITY

Schedules are like pinatas.
Their ultimate destiny
is to be broken.

154

STRESS OR SANITY

With all the modern conveniences
available, it's now possible
to have a bad day and
never leave the house.

155

STRESS OR SANITY

Under pressure, eggs crack
and coal turns into diamonds.
The same can be said for people.

156

STRESS OR SANITY

A traffic report is generally given by someone who is flying over the parking lot you're already stuck in.

157

STRESS OR SANITY

If ignorance is bliss,
I must be a very happy person.

158

**Stressful Situation #46:
A new white carpet and a puppy.**

STRESS OR SANITY

If I could figure out a way
to fax my kids to daycare,
I'd save 45 minutes per day.

160

STRESS OR SANITY

Staff Infection: When the whole office catches Spring Fever.

161

STRESS OR SANITY

When it rains, it pours...generally into the windows you left open.

162

STRESS OR SANITY

Stress is caused by saying,
"No problem" when we mean,
"No chance."

163

STRESS OR SANITY

**Man does not live by bread alone.
Sometimes he wants a beer, too.**

164

STRESS OR SANITY

Hard work is its own reward,
but wouldn't you rather
have the money?

165

STRESS OR SANITY

The term "working mother" is redundant.

166

STRESS OR SANITY

#1 on the Best Stressed List:
The guy whose ex-wife just
got her law degree.

167

OTHER TITLES BY GREAT QUOTATIONS

201 Best Things Ever Said
A Lifetime Of Love
A Light Heart Lives Long
A Teacher Is Better Than Two Books
The ABC's Of Parenting
As A Cat Thinketh
The Best Of Friends
The Birthday Astrologer
Cheatnotes On Life
Chicken Soup
Dear Mr. President
Don't Deliberate…Litigate
Fantastic Father, Dependable Dad
For Mother—A Bouquet Of Sentiments
Global Wisdom
Golden Years, Golden Words
Grandma, I Love You
Growing Up In Toyland
Happiness Is Found Along The Way
Heal The World
Hollywords
Hooked On Golf
I'm Not Over The Hill
In Celebration Of Women
Inspirations—Compelling Food For Thought

Interior Design For Idiots
Let's Talk Decorating
Life's Simple Pleasures
Money For Nothing, Tips For Free
Motivating Quotes For Motivated People
Mrs. Aesop's Fables
Mrs. Murphy's Laws
Mrs. Webster's Dictionary
Mrs. Webster's Guide To Business
Parenting 101
Real Estate Agents And Their
 Dirty Little Tricks
Reflections
Romantic Rhapsody
The Secret Language Of Men
The Secret Language Of Women
Some Things Never Change
The Sports Page
Stress Or Sanity
TeenAge Of Insanity
Thanks From The Heart
Things You'll Learn, If You Live
 Long Enough
Wedding Wonders
Women On Men

GREAT QUOTATIONS PUBLISHING COMPANY
1967 Quincy Court
Glendale Heights, IL 60139-2045
Phone (630) 582-2800
Fax (630) 582-2813